# silly Millies

# I AM A PENCIL

BIG YELLOW

Linda Hayward

Illustrations by Carol Nicklaus

The Millbrook Press  Brookfield, Connecticut

# FOR JAN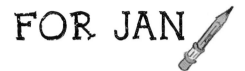

Copyright © 2003 by Linda Hayward
Illustrations copyright © 2003 by Carol Nicklaus

Reading Consultant: Lea M. McGee, Ed. D.

Silly Millies and the Silly Millies logo are trademarks
of The Millbrook Press, Inc.

Library of Congress Cataloging-in-Publication Data

Hayward, Linda.
I am a pencil / Linda Hayward ; illustrations by Carol Nicklaus.
p. cm.—(Silly Millies)
Summary: Describes how a pencil is manufactured, distributed, and used.
ISBN 0-7613-2904-8 (lib. bdg.)      ISBN 0-7613-1825-9 (pbk.)
1. Pencils—Juvenile literature.   [1. Pencils.   2. Pencil industry.]
I. Nicklaus, Carol, ill.   II. Title.   III. Series.
TS1268.H39 2003
674'.88—dc21      2002014847

Published by The Millbrook Press, Inc.
2 Old New Milford Road
Brookfield, Connecticut 06804
www.millbrookpress.com

I am a pencil. I was made to write. But here I am, stuck in a kid's box with a stapler, some scissors, and a bunch of crayons.

Get me out of here!

I want to leave my mark.

I want to tell my story.

BIG YELLOW

Case

Look at me.

See my long wood coat.

The folks who made me call
it a case.

But what do they know about the
hopes and dreams of a pencil like me?

See my dark gray core.

It is as long as my wood coat.

I could draw circles around everybody
if I only had a point.

My hat is a cute little red eraser.

Core

But what good is an eraser when there is nothing to erase?

Eraser

7

I did not start off looking this good.
Before I was a pencil, I was just a
skinny stick of graphite.
Graphite is a mineral that makes a black
mark on paper.

Sure, I could write.
But I could break, too.
And I was messy.
I could leave smudges
on the hand that held me.
I needed a new look.

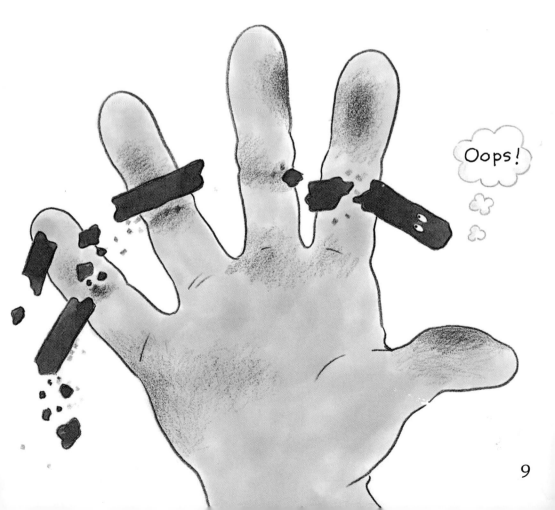

My story begins in a big hole in
the ground—a quarry.
This quarry is full of rocks.
The rocks have graphite in them.

Miners scrape away the dirt and rock
to find the graphite.
It has been there for millions of years.
How cool! I go way back.
A truck takes the graphite
to the pencil factory.

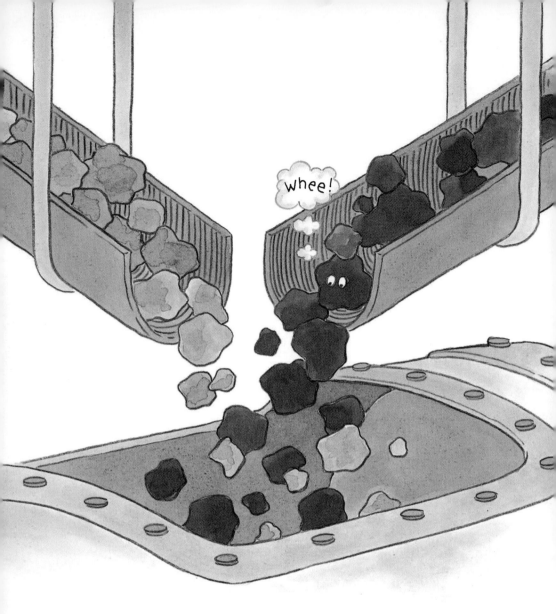

At the factory the chunks of graphite are mixed with clay. Clay helps make graphite hard.

Next the graphite and clay are ground into powder.

Wow!

Then the dark gray powder is turned
into paste.
The paste is squeezed through a tube.
Yeek! Becoming a pencil is no walk
in the park.

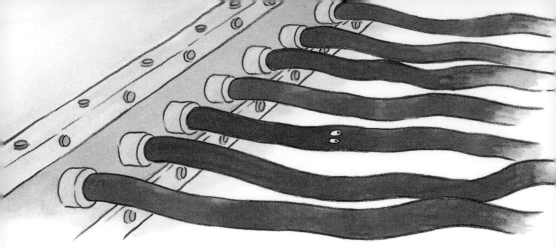

My graphite center comes out of the tube
as part of a really long stick.
The stick is cut into pieces.

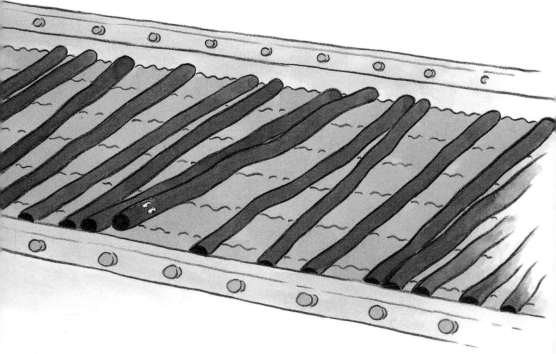

There I am—the piece in the middle—about
to get baked in an oven.
It is hot inside the oven.
The heat makes me hard and smooth.

Next stop, the groover!
I take the forklift.
I have a little time to think
about all the stuff I want
to write about someday.

16

At the groover, I am laid on a block of cedar.

Cedar is a hard wood that does not splinter.

The cedar block has ten grooves in it.

I fit into one of them.

Nine more sticks of graphite are

in the other grooves.

Groove

A gluing machine glues another
block of cedar on top of us.

How
cozy!

Now I am part of a graphite
sandwich!

A cutting machine cuts the sandwich into ten separate pencils.
That is how I get my long wood coat.

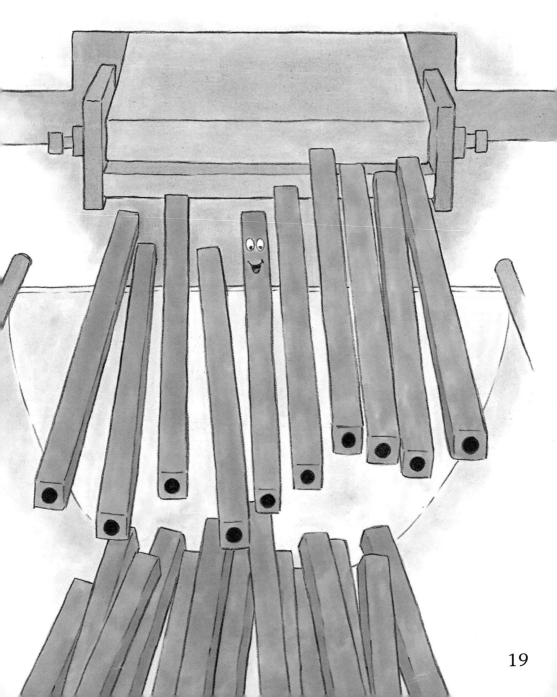

A trimming machine trims me.
Now I have six sides.
Lay me down, and I will not roll
away like some roll-about crayon.

A sanding machine sands me.
Now I am smooth enough to hold.

The painting machine is next.
This is when I really start to shine.
I go through it again and again
until I am a beautiful yellow.

BIG YELLOW    2

BIG YELLOW    2

BIG YELLOW    2

BIG YELLOW    2

Next I get stamped with some
letters and a number.
The number tells how dark I will write.
A number 2 means my mark is plenty dark.

22

Now the banding machine presses
a metal band around my top end.
Next I will get my hat.

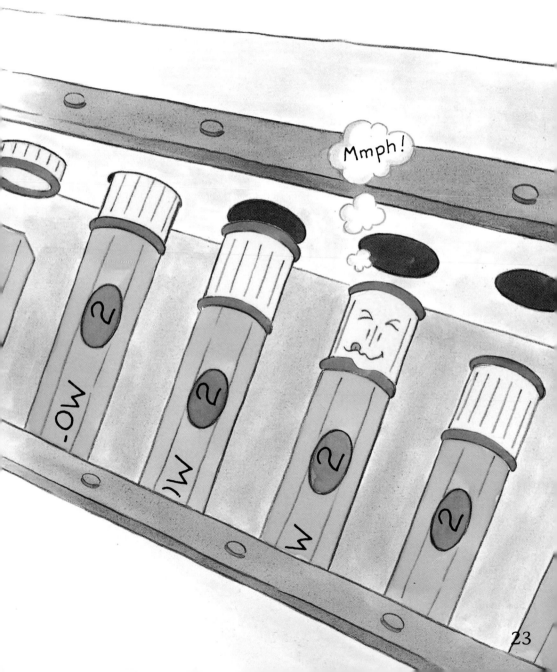

The machine fills the band with glue.
Then it pushes in a little red eraser.
The eraser goes in, but it cannot
fall out.

Ta–daaa! I am ready for the world.
The factory folks put me in a
cardboard box with other pencils.

They put the boxes in a carton.
They load the cartons on a truck.

The truck ride is a bit bumpy.
We start. We stop.

We go fast. We go slow.

I am glad when that ride is over.

The truck is opened.

One carton is taken out of the truck.

What is going on?

The box I am in is taken out
of the carton.
The box is opened up.
Oh, look. I am in a room full
of kids—a classroom.
I am given to someone. Lucky me!
That is how I wound up in this kid's box.

Now that someone is
picking me up.
My dream is coming true.
That someone takes me to
the pencil sharpener.
Oooh. It tickles.
But it feels good to
be sharpened . . .
if you are a pencil.

At last!

YELLOW

2

Now look at me.

Do you see my point?

I am one sharp writing tool.

I can go anywhere.

I work without batteries.

I do not have to be plugged in.

I will not crash.

I want to tell everything.
I want to do doodles.
Just show me some paper.

**Dear Parents:**

Congratulations! By sharing this book with your child, you are helping your child become a lifelong reader. *I Am a Pencil* is perfect for the child who is beginning to read alone. Below are some ideas for making sure your child's reading experience is a positive one.

**TIPS FOR READING:**
- Your child may be able to read this book alone. However, children enjoy reading even more when they read a new book aloud with a parent. If your child is unsure about a word, ask your child to point to the parts of the word he or she knows (your child will likely know the sounds of beginning and ending letters and some familiar word parts found in frequently occurring words). If your child is stumped, read the word slowly, pointing to each letter as you sound out the word. Don't worry if your child stumbles on words for unfamiliar objects or animals. This book is designed to help your child learn new vocabulary. Always provide lots of praise for your child's hard work.
- *I Am a Pencil* is written to present your child with interesting new information. Stop to comment on a fact that is new to you. Engage your child in discussion about the book's pictures and unusual information as you read together.
- Encourage your child to reread the book again. Rereading, silently and aloud, helps children learn to read words more quickly and fluently.

**TIPS FOR DISCUSSION:**
- It's fun to think about how things are made. Even a mud pie needs to be made in a certain order. What are the steps in making a mud pie? Or a real pie? How about a book?
- This book includes many cause and effect relationships. For example: Clay is added to graphite BECAUSE the clay makes the graphite harder. See how many cause and effects you and your child can locate together.
- This book makes clear that a pencil is a useful tool. Challenge your child to think why a pencil is sometimes better than a pen or a marker.

Lea M. McGee, Ed.D.
**Professor, Literacy Education**
**University of Alabama**